W I T H D R A W N

WORN, SOILED, OBSOLETE

SHAWLS TWO

SHAWLS TWO

SIXTH&SPRING BOOKS
NEW YORK

SIXTH&SPRING BOOKS
233 Spring Street
New York, New York 10013

Library of Congress Control Number: 2008925411

ISBN-10: 1-933027-65-7
ISBN-13: 978-1-933027-65-4

Manufactured in China

3 5 7 9 10 8 6 4

First Edition, 2008

TABLE OF CONTENTS

20   **FRINGED SHAWL**
Drape expectations

24   **TEXTURED SHAWL**
Fringe benefits

26   **TIED SHAWLETTE**
Gossamer dream

29   **BEADED LEAF LACE SHAWL**
Rhapsody in red

36   **WAVE-PATTERN SHAWL**
In the limelight

38   **STAINED GLASS WINDOW SHAWL**
Check it out

42   **SEED-STITCH SHAWL**
Bermuda triangle

44   **ZIGZAG LACE SHAWL**
Diamonds are forever

48   **DOUBLE DIAMOND SHAWL**
Scarborough fair

52   **RUFFLED CAPELET**
Short 'n sweet

55   **DROP-STITCH SHAWL**
Pink champagne

58   **SCALLOP-STITCH WRAP**
Amazing grays

60   **CABLED WRAP**
Ivy league

64   **TEXTURED ZIGZAG SHAWL**
Catch some zzz's

67   **SHORT-ROW SHAWL**
Tree hugger

70   **TRIANGULAR GARTER-STITCH SHAWL**
Midas touch

72   **TANGO SHAWL**
Red hot

74   **MOHAIR AND RIBBON WRAP**
Forest path

76   **MULTI-YARN WRAP**
Special blend

79   **WAVE AND LEAF SHAWL**
Milk and honey

84   **FLOWERS AND SNOWFLAKES SHAWL**
Blue Danube

88   **AFGHAN SHAWL**
Teal's good

INTRODUCTION

There were too many gorgeous designs to fit into one book of shawls, so we had to create a second! *Shawls Two* is chock-full of fabulous new projects to keep your needles busy and your shoulders warm all year long.

Shawls run the gamut from simple to sumptuous, cuddly to elegant, casual to dressy, making them among the most versatile garments to wear and to knit. You'll find a shawl in this book for every style and occasion.

Whether you're going out on the town or curling up on the couch, *Shawls Two* has the perfect wrap to do it in style. Tango the night away in a dazzling red flame-stitch shawl that glimmers with gold glass beads (page 29). Chase away the chill with a luxe cashmere shawl that features an elegant looped I-cord edging (page 58). Make a statement with a mohair-blend wrap of colorful blocks bordered by strips of black (page 38) or get your flirt on in a charming ruffled capelet knit with variegated yarns (page 52).

All knitters, from beginners to more advanced stitchers, will delight in these irresistible patterns created by some of today's top knitwear designers. So grab your needles and get ready to knit **ON THE GO!**

THE BASICS

Shawls have been worn for thousands of years to keep the wearer warm, as a fashion accessory and for symbolic reasons. Today, shawls are as popular as ever, and the styles available are as diverse as the women who wear them. For knitters looking to stretch their skills, a shawl is the perfect next step up from a basic scarf, because shawls require very little, if any, shaping and are usually one-size-fits-all. Most shawls are based on one of three simple shapes—square, rectangle and triangle—but the designs can vary from a basic garter-stitch triangle to a complex wrap with multiple lace patterns. We have included shawls in a range of styles and skill levels to tempt every knitter.

SIZING

Most of the shawls in this book are written in one size. If you are not sure if the size given in the pattern will fit you, then look at the "Knitted Measurements" at the beginning of the pattern, cut or fold a piece of fabric to those measurements, try it on, and adjust from there. It is relatively easy to change the measurements. If the style is a simple rectangle or square, cast on more or fewer stitches to the cast-on to alter the width (pay attention to the stitch multiple, if necessary), and work fewer or more rows to alter the length. For a triangle shape, it is a more involved process. If the triangle begins at the widest point, you will have to adjust the cast-on number. First determine the desired width and alter the number of cast-on stitches accordingly. Then decide on the length to the point, calculate the number of rows needed to get to the point and work the decreases evenly over this number of rows. Of course, if the triangle is worked from the point up, you still need to determine the width and length, but reverse the shaping. That is, cast on the same number of stitches as in the original pattern and adjust the number of pattern repeats. Also note that if you adjust any pattern from the original, you may need to alter the yarn amount.

CONSTRUCTION

There is very little to the construction of most shawls, as they are usually worked in one piece with little or no shaping. However, some more complicated patterns have more than one piece, such as the Flowers and Snowflakes Shawl on page 84. It is best to use a circular needle for those versions worked

GAUGE

It is always important to knit a gauge swatch, and it is even more so with garments to ensure proper fit.

Patterns usually state gauge over a 4"/10cm span; however, it's beneficial to make a larger test swatch. This gives you a more precise stitch gauge, a better idea of the appearance and drape of the knitted fabric, and a chance to familiarize yourself with the stitch pattern.

The type of needles used—straight or circular, wood or metal—will influence gauge, so knit your swatch with the needles you plan to use for the project. Measure gauge as illustrated. Try different needle sizes until your sample measures the required number of stitches and rows. *To get fewer stitches to the inch/cm, use larger needles; to get more stitches to the inch/cm, use smaller needles.*

Knitting in the round may tighten the gauge, so if you measured the gauge on a flat swatch, take another gauge reading after you begin knitting. When the piece measures at least 2"/5cm, lay it flat and measure over the stitches in the center of the piece, as the side stitches may be distorted.

It's a good idea to keep your gauge swatch, in order to test blocking and cleaning methods.

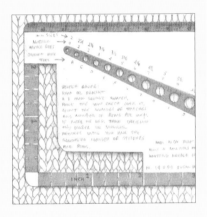

horizontally, to easily accommodate the large number of stitches. Some triangle shawls are knit from the point up, thereby allowing you to try on the piece while knitting and adjust the length to your liking, such as the Triangular Garter-Stitch Shawl on page 70.

YARN SELECTION

To reproduce the projects exactly as they are shown in this book, use the yarn listed in the Materials section of the patterns. We've chosen yarns that are readily available in the U.S. and Canada at the time of printing. The Resources list on pages 90 and 91 provides addresses of yarn distributors. Contact them for the name of a retailer in your area.

YARN SUBSTITUTION

You may wish to substitute yarns. Perhaps

Categories of yarn, gauge ranges, and recommended needle and hook sizes

Yarn Weight Symbol & Category Names	1 Super Fine	2 Fine	3 Light	4 Medium	5 Bulky	6 Super Bulky
Type of Yarns in Category	Sock, Fingering, Baby	Sport, Baby	DK, Light Worsted	Worsted, Afghan, Aran	Chunky, Craft, Rug	Bulky, Roving
Knit Gauge Range* in Stockinette Stitch to 4 Inches	27–32 sts	23–26 sts	21–24 sts	16–20 sts	12–15 sts	6–11 sts
Recommended Needle in Metric Size Range	2.25–3.25 mm	3.25–3.75 mm	3.75–4.5 mm	4.5–5.5 mm	5.5–8 mm	8 mm and larger
Recommended Needle U.S. Size Range	1 to 3	3 to 5	5 to 7	7 to 9	9 to 11	11 and larger
Crochet Gauge* Ranges in Single Crochet to 4 Inches	21–32 sts	16–20 sts	12–17 sts	11–14 sts	8–11 sts	5–9 sts
Recommended Hook in Metric Size Range	2.25–3.5 mm	3.5–4.5 mm	4.5–5.5 mm	5.5–6.5 mm	6.5–9 mm	9 mm and larger
Recommended Hook U.S. Size Range	B–1 to E–4	E–4 to 7	7 to I–9	I–9 to K–10½	K–10½ to M–13	M–13 and larger

*Guidelines only: The above reflects the most commonly used needle or hook sizes for specific yarn categories.

■□□□

Beginner

Ideal first project.

■■□□

Easy

Basic stitches, minimal shaping, simple finishing.

■■■□

Intermediate

For knitters with some experience. More intricate stitches, shaping, and finishing.

■■■■

Experienced

For knitters able to work patterns with complicated shaping and finishing.

you view small-scale projects as a chance to use up leftovers from your yarn stash, or maybe the yarn specified is not available in your area. You'll need to knit to the given gauge to obtain the knitted measurements with a substitute yarn (see "Gauge," on page 11). Be sure to consider how the fiber content of the substitute yarn will affect the comfort and the ease of care of your projects.

To facilitate your substitution, this book gives the standard yarn weight for each yarn. You'll find a yarn weight symbol in the Materials section of the pattern, immediately following the color of the yarn. Look for a substitute yarn that falls into the same category. The suggested needle size and gauge on the yarn label should be comparable to those on the Standard Yarn Weight System chart (see page 12).

After you've successfully gauge-swatched a substitute yarn, you'll need to figure out how much of the substitute yarn the project requires. First, find the total length of the original yarn in the pattern (multiply number of balls by yards/meters per ball). Divide this figure by the new yards/meters per ball (listed on the yarn label). Round up to the next whole number. The answer is the number of balls required.

FOLLOWING CHARTS

Charts are a convenient way to follow colorwork, lace, cable, and other stitch patterns at a glance. The charts in this book utilize the universal knitting language of "symbolcraft." When knitting back and forth in rows, read charts from right to left on right side (RS) rows and from left to right on wrong side (WS) rows, repeating any stitch and row repeats as directed in the pattern. When knitting in the round, read charts from right to left on every round. Posting a self-adhesive note under your working row is an easy way to keep track of your place on a chart.

BLOCKING

Blocking is an all-important finishing step in the knitting process. It is the best way to shape pattern pieces and smooth knitted edges in preparation for seaming or for a neat and even edge. If you have no seams and the fabric is already smooth and even, blocking may not be necessary. However, if you do want to block an item that was knit in the round, lay it flat and block the double thickness, being careful not to make creases if using an iron. Most items retain their shape if the blocking stages in the instructions are followed carefully. Choose a blocking method according to the yarn-care label and when in doubt, test-block your gauge swatch.

Wet Block Method

Using rust-proof pins, pin pieces to measurements on a flat surface and lightly dampen using a spray bottle. Allow to dry before removing pins.

Steam Block Method

With WS facing, pin pieces. Steam lightly,

holding the iron 2"/5cm above the knitting. Do not press or it will flatten stitches.

FINISHING

After blocking, there is usually very little, if any, finishing on a shawl. Sometimes fringe is added onto the ends. You can make the fringe as short or long as you like, depending on preference or amount of leftover yarn. A crocheted edge can also be added to keep the edges from curling.

SEWING

When using a very bulky or highly textured yarn, it is sometimes easier to seam pieces together with a finer, flat yarn. Just be sure that your sewing yarn closely matches the color of the original yarn used in your project.

CARE

Refer to the yarn label for the recommended cleaning method. Many of the projects in the book can be either washed by hand or in the machine on a gentle or wool cycle, in lukewarm water with a mild detergent. Do not agitate or soak for more than ten minutes. Rinse gently with tepid water, then fold in a towel and gently squeeze out the water. Lay flat to dry away from excess heat and light. Check the yarn label for any specific care instructions, such as dry cleaning or tumble drying.

WORKING A YARN OVER

Between two knit stitches: Bring the yarn from the back of the work to the front between the two needles. Knit the next stitch, bringing the yarn to the back over the right-hand needle, as shown.

TASSELS

Cut a piece of cardboard to the desired length of the tassel. Wrap yarn around the cardboard. Knot a piece of yarn tightly around one end, cut as shown, and remove the cardboard. Wrap and tie yarn around the tassel about 1"/2.5cm down from the top to secure the fringe.

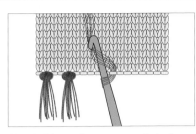

Simple fringe: Cut yarn twice desired length, plus extra for knotting. On WS, insert hook from front to back through piece and over folded yarn. Pull yarn through. Draw ends through and tighten. Trim yarn.

Knotted fringe: After working a simple fringe (it should be longer to allow for extra knotting), take one-half of the strands from each fringe and knot them with half the strands from the neighboring fringe.

1 Make a slip knot on the left needle. *Insert the right needle knitwise into the stitch on the left needle. Wrap the yarn around the right needle as if to knit.

2 Draw the yarn through the first stitch to make a new stitch, but do not drop the stitch from the left needle.

3 Slip the new stitch to the left needle as shown. Repeat from the * until the required number of stitches is cast on.

CABLE CAST-ON

The cable cast-on forms a sturdy elastic edge. it is perfect for ribbed edges.

 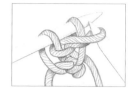 

I Cast on two stitches using the knit-on cast-on as described on page 15. *Insert the right needle between the two stithes on the left needle.

2 Wrap the yarn around the right needle as if to knit and pull the yarn through to make a new stitch.

3 Place the new stitch on the left needle as shown. Repeat from the *, always inserting the right needle in between the last two stitches on the left needle.

THREE-NEEDLE BIND-OFF

This bind-off is used to join two edges that have the same number of stitches, such as shoulder edges, which have been placed on holders.

I With the right side of the two pieces facing each other, and the needles parallel, insert a third needle knitwise into the first stitch of each needle. Wrap the yarn around the needle as if to knit.

2 Knit these two stitches together and slip them off the needles. *Knit the next two stitches together in the same way as shown.

3 Slip the first stitch on the third needle over the second stitch and off the needle. Repeat from the * in step 2 across the row until all the stitches are bound off.

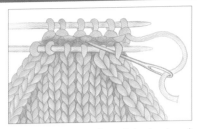

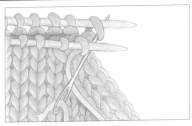

1 Insert tapestry needle purlwise (as shown) through first stitch on front needle. Pull yarn through, leaving that stitch on knitting needle.

2 Insert tapestry needle knitwise (as shown) through first stitch on back needle. Pull yarn through, leaving stitch on knitting needle.

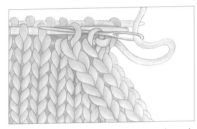

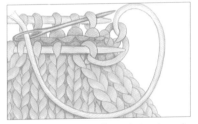

3 Insert tapestry needle knitwise through first stitch on front needle, slip stitch off needle and insert tapestry needle purlwise (as shown) through next stitch on front needle. Pull yarn through, leaving this stitch on needle.

4 Insert tapestry needle purlwise through first stitch on back needle. Slip stitch off needle and insert tapestry needle knitwise (as shown) through next stitch on back needle. Pull yarn through, leaving this stitch on needle.

Repeat steps 3 and 4 until all stitches on both front and back needles have been grafted. Fasten off and weave in end.

CROCHET STITCHES

CHAIN

I Pass the yarn over the hook and catch it with the hook.

2 Draw the yarn through the loop on the hook.

3 Repeat steps 1 and 2 to make a chain.

SINGLE CROCHET

I Insert the hook through top two loops of a stitch. Pass the yarn over the hook and draw up a loop—two loops on hook.

2 Pass the yarn over the hook and draw through both loops on hook.

3 Continue in the same way, inserting the hook into each stitch.

HALF-DOUBLE CROCHET

I Pass the yarn over the hook. Insert the hook through the top two loops of a stitch.

2 Pass the yarn over the hook and draw up a loop—three loops on hook. Pass the yarn over the hook.

3 Draw through all three loops on hook.

DOUBLE CROCHET

I Pass the yarn over the hook. Insert the hook through the top two loops of a stitch.

2 Pass the yarn over the hook and draw up a loop— three loops on hook.

SLIP STITCH

Insert the crochet hook into a stitch, catch the yarn, and pull up a loop. Draw the loop through the loop on the hook.

3 Pass the yarn over the hook and draw it through the first two loops on the hook, pass the yarn over the hook and draw through the remaining two loops. Continue in the same way, inserting the hook into each stitch.

Illustrations: Joni Coniglio

KNITTING TERMS AND ABBREVIATIONS

approx approximately

beg begin(ning)

bind off Used to finish an edge and keep stitches from unraveling. Lift the first stitch over the second, the second over the third, etc. (UK: cast off)

cast on A foundation row of stitches placed on the needle in order to begin knitting.

CC contrast color

ch chain(s)

cm centimeter(s)

cn cable needle

cont continu(e)(ing)

dc double crochet (UK: tr–treble)

dec decrease(ing)—Reduce the stitches in a row (knit 2 together).

dpn double pointed needle(s)

foll follow(s)(ing)

g gram(s)

garter stitch Knit every row. Circular knitting: Knit one round, then purl one round.

hdc half-double crochet (UK: htr–half treble)

inc increase(ing)—Add stitches in a row (knit into the front and back of a stitch).

k knit

k2tog knit 2 stitches together

lp(s) loops(s)

LH left-hand

m meter(s)

M1 make one stitch—With the needle tip, lift the strand between last stitch worked and next stitch on the left-hand needle and knit into the back of it. One stitch has been added.

MC main color

mm millimeter(s)

oz ounce(s)

p purl

p2tog purl 2 stitches together

pat pattern

pick up and knit (purl) Knit (or purl) into the loops along an edge.

pm place marker—Place or attach a loop of contrast yarn or purchased stitch marker as indicated.

rem remain(s)(ing)

rep repeat

rev St st reverse Stockinette stitch—Purl right-side rows, knit wrong-side rows. Circular knitting: Purl all rounds. (UK: reverse stocking stitch)

rnd(s) round(s)

RH right-hand

RS right side(s)

sc single crochet (UK: dc–double crochet)

sk skip

SKP Slip 1, knit 1, pass slip stitch over knit 1.

SK2P Slip 1, knit 2 together, pass slip stitch over k2tog.

sl slip—An unworked stitch made by passing a stitch from the left-hand to the right-hand needle as if to purl.

sl st slip stitch (UK: single crochet)

ssk slip, slip, knit—Slip next 2 stitches knitwise, one at a time, to right-hand needle. Insert tip of left-hand needle into fronts of these stitches from left to right. Knit them together. One stitch has been decreased.

st(s) stitch(es)

St st Stockinette stitch—Knit right-side rows, purl wrong-side rows. Circular knitting: Knit all rounds. (UK: stocking stitch)

tbl through back of loop

tog together

tr treble crochet (UK: dtr–double treble)

WS wrong side(s)

w&t wrap and turn

wyif with yarn in front

wyib with yarn in back

work even Continue in pattern without increasing or decreasing. (UK: work straight)

yd yard(s)

yo yarn over—Make a new stitch by wrapping the yarn over the right-hand needle. (UK: yfwd, yon, yrn)

* Repeat directions following * as many times as indicated.

[ ] Repeat directions inside brackets as many times as indicated.

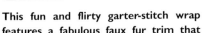

This fun and flirty garter-stitch wrap features a fabulous faux fur trim that accentuates the ruffled bottom edge. Designed by Laura Bryant.

SIZES
Instructions are written for one size.

KNITTED MEASUREMENTS
- Width across top edge approx 54"/137cm
- Width across bottom edge approx 158"/401.5cm
- Length from neck to bottom approx 19"/48cm

MATERIALS
- 7 2oz/57g hanks (each approx 92yd/82m) of Prism Yarns *Indulgence* (silk/wool/kid mohair/nylon) in moss (MC) 🔟
- 5 2oz/57g hanks (each approx 45yd/40m) of Prism Yarns *Fern* (nylon) in moss (CC) 🔟
- One pair size 10 (6mm) needles *or size to obtain gauge*
- One size 17 (12.75mm) needle (for binding off)
- Size 10 and 13 (6 and 9mm) circular needles, 36"/91cm long
- Size H/8 (5mm) crochet hook

GAUGE
16 sts and 28 rows to 4"/10cm over garter st using size 10 (6mm) needles and MC. *Take time to check gauge.*

Notes
1 Wrap is made vertically from right top corner to left top corner.
2 Back section is shaped using short-row wrapping.

SHORT-ROW WRAPPING
(wrap and turn—w&t)
1 Work specified number of sts.
2 Wyif, slip next st knitwise onto RH needle.
3 Wyib, slip st back onto LH needle (one wrapped st), turn and work back specified number of sts.
Note There is no need to pick up the wrapped sts on subsequent rows because the wraps blend in with the garter sts.

SHAWL
With MC, cast on 1 st.
Inc row 1 row (RS) K in front, back and front of st—3 sts. Knit next row.
Inc row 2 (RS) K to last st, k in front and back of last st (inc made)—4 sts.
Working in garter st, rep inc row 2 every other row 16 times more, then every 4th row 16 times, end with a RS row—36 sts.
Beg Short-Row Shaping
Row 1 (WS) K6, w&t; knit to end.
Row 2 K12, w&t; knit to end.
Row 3 K18, w&t; knit to end.
Row 4 K24, w&t; knit to end.
Row 5 K30, w&t; knit to end.
Row 6 Knit across all sts.

Row (inc) 7 (RS) K to last st, inc in last st—37 sts.

Rows 8–12 Rep rows 1–5.

Row 13 K36, w&t; knit to end.

Row 14 Knit across all sts.

Row (inc) 15 (RS) K to last st, inc in last st—38 sts.

Rep rows 8–15 5 times more—43 sts.

Rows 16–21 Rep rows 8–13.

Row 22 K42, w&t; knit to end.

Row 23 Knit across all sts.

Row (inc) 24 (RS) K to last st, inc in last st—44 sts.

Rep rows 16–24 5 times more—49 sts.

Rows 25–31 Rep rows 16–22.

Row 32 K48, w&t; knit to end.

Row 33 Knit across all sts.

Row (inc) 34 (RS) K to last st, inc in last st—50 sts.

Rep rows 25–34 4 times more—54 sts.

Rows 35–42 Rep rows 25–32.

Rows 43 and 44 Knit across all sts.

Rep rows 35–44 twice more.

Beg Reverse Short-Row Shaping

Row 1 (WS) K48, w&t; knit to end.

Row 2 K42, w&t; knit to end.

Row 3 K36, w&t; knit to end.

Row 4 K30, w&t; knit to end.

Row 5 K24, w&t; knit to end.

Row 6 K18, w&t; knit to end.

Row 7 K12, w&t; knit to end.

Row 8 K6, w&t; knit to end.

Rows 9 and 10 Knit across all sts.

Rep rows 1–10 once more, then rows 1–9 once.

Row (dec) 11 (RS) K to last 2 sts, k2tog—53 sts.

Rows 12–19 Rep rows 1–8.

Row 20 Knit across all sts.

Row (dec) 21 (RS) K to last 2 sts, k2tog—52 sts.

Rep rows 12–21 4 times more—48 sts.

Rows 22–28 Rep rows 2–8.

Row 29 Knit across all sts.

Row (dec) 30 (RS) K to last 2 sts, k2tog—47 sts.

Rep rows 22–30 5 times more—42 sts.

Rows 31–36 Rep rows 3–8.

Row 37 Knit across all sts.

Row (dec) 38 (RS) K to last 2 sts, k2tog—41 sts.

Rep rows 31–38 5 times more—36 sts.

Rows 39–43 Rep rows 4–8.

Next row Knit across all sts.

Dec row 1 (RS) K to last 2 sts, k2tog—35 sts.

Rep dec row 1 every 4th row 15 times more, then every other row 16 times, end with a WS row—3 sts.

Dec row 2 (RS) K3tog. Fasten off last st.

FAUX FUR TRIM

With RS facing, smaller circular needle and CC, pick up and k 438 sts evenly spaced (approx 1 st in every other row) along entire curved bottom edge. Change to larger circular needle.

Next row (WS) K3, *yo, k3; rep from * to end—583 sts. Knit next row.

Next row (WS) K4, *yo, k3; rep from * to end—776 sts. Knit next 2 rows.

Bind off as foll: with size 17 (12.75mm) needle, MC and working very loosely, k first st; with CC, k next st; pass MC st on RH needle over CC st; *with MC, k next st, pass CC st on RH needle over MC st; with CC, k next st, pass MC st on RH needle over CC st; rep from * to end.

EDGING

With RS facing and crochet hook, join MC with a sl st in top RH edge.

Row 1 (RS) Ch 1, sc in same place st joining, making sure that work lies flat, sc evenly across entire top edge. Do *not* turn.

Row 2 Ch 1, working from *left to right*, sc in each st across. Fasten off.

TEXTURED SHAWL
Fringe benefits

Knitted fringe adds flair to this generously sized shawl, while a simple broken rib-stitch creates the overall fabric. Designed by Pauline Schultz.

SIZES
Instructions are written for one size.

KNITTED MEASUREMENTS
■ Approx 27"/68.5cm wide x 72"/183cm long (excluding fringe)

MATERIALS
■ 14 2.8oz/80g skeins (each approx 145yd/133m) of Moda Dea/Coats & Clark Bamboo Wool (rayon from bamboo/ wool) in #3530 periwinkle
■ Size 8 (5mm) circular needle, 24"/60cm long or size to obtain gauge
■ Size H/8 (5mm) crochet hook
■ Contrasting worsted weight yarn (waste yarn)

GAUGE
20 sts and 27½ rows to 4"/10cm over pat st using size 8 (5mm) circular needle.
Take time to check gauge.

STITCH GLOSSARY
Cable cast-on Cast on 2 sts. *Insert RH needle between the 2 sts on LH needle. Wrap yarn around RH needle as if to knit and pull yarn through to make a new st. Place new st on LH needle. Rep from * always inserting RH needle in between the last 2 sts on LH needle and until required number of sts is achieved.

PATTERN STITCH
(over an even number of sts)
Row 1 (RS) Sl 1, k to end.
Row 2 Rep row 1.
Rows 3 and 4 Sl 1, *k1, p1; rep from *, end k1.
Rep rows 1–4 for pat st.

SHAWL
With crochet hook and waste yarn, ch 143. Cut yarn and draw end though lp on hook. Turn ch so bottom lps are at top and cut end is at LH side. With circular needles, beg 2 lps from opposite end, pick up and k 1 st in each of next 136 lps. Do *not* join. Work back and forth in pat st until piece measures approx 71"/180.5cm from beg (121 pat reps), end with a WS row. Rep rows 1 and 2.

FRINGE
Beg with first st on LH needle, *bind off 1 st, place st back on LH needle, then cable cast-on 19 sts (20 sts on needle). Knit 1 row. Purl 1 row. Bind off 21 sts knitwise. Rep from * across; bind off last st. To add fringe to opposite end, work as foll: with RS facing, release cut end from lp of waste yarn ch. Pull out 1 ch at a time, placing each st on LH needle. Rep rows 1 and 2 of pat st. Work fringe from ** to ** as for first end.

FINISHING
Block piece to measurements.

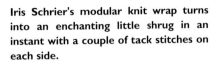

Iris Schrier's modular knit wrap turns into an enchanting little shrug in an instant with a couple of tack stitches on each side.

Instructions are written for size Small. Changes for Medium and Large are in parentheses.

KNITTED MEASUREMENTS

■ Length from neck to bottom edge 11 (12¼, 14)"/28 (31, 35.5)cm

MATERIALS

■ 2 1¾oz/50g hanks (each approx 163yd/ 149m) of Artyarns *Regal Silk* (silk) in #101 purple mix (A)

■ 1 1¾oz/50g hank (approx 510yd/ 466m) of Artyarns *Beaded Cashmere 1* (cashmere) in #101 purple mix (B)

■ One 4"/10cm wide x 60"/152.5cm Artyarns Silk Hand-Dyed Scarf in color #101

■ Size 8 (5mm) circular needle, 24"/60cm long *or size to obtain gauge*

■ Stitch holder

■ Stitch marker

■ Large-eye yarn needle

GAUGE

10 sts and 22 rows to 4"/10cm over garter st using size 8 (5mm) circular needle.
Take time to check gauge.

Notes

1 Shawl is made in one piece from the bottom up.

2 Shawl is divided into three sections that form the angular shape.

STITCH GLOSSARY

Inc 1 st K in front and back of st.

Knitting-On (for cast on) *Knit next stitch on LN but do not drop stitch from needle. Slip new stitch from RN to LN— *one stitch cast-on;* rep from* for number of desired sts.

SHAWLETTE

Back section

With A, cast on 3 sts.

Row 1 (RS) K1, inc 1 st, p1—4 sts.

Row 2 [Inc 1 st] twice, pm, k1, p1—6 sts. Change to B.

Row 3 With B, inc 1 st, k to marker, drop marker, inc 1 st, pm, k to last st, end p1—8 sts.

Row 4 Rep row 3—10 sts. Change to A.

Rows 5 and 6 With A, rep row 3. Change to B.

Rep rows 3–6 until there are 76 (84, 96) sts on needle.

Side section 1

Next row (RS) With B, k 37 (41, 47), p1, drop marker, place rem 38 (42, 48) sts on holder for side section 2.

Next row K to last st, end p1. Change to A.

Rows 1 and 2 With A, k to last st, end p1. Change to B.

Rows 3 and 4 With B, k to last st, end p1. Change to A.

Rep rows 1–4 5 (9, 13) times more. With A, cast on 38 (42, 48) sts using the knitting-on method.

Next row K37 (41, 47), k2tog, pm, k to last 2 sts, end p2tog. Change to B.

Rows 1 and 2 With B, k to marker, drop marker, k2tog, pm, k to last 2 sts, end p2tog. Change to A.

Rows 3 and 4 With A, k to marker, drop marker, k2tog, pm, k to last 2 sts, end p2tog.

Rep rows 1–4 until there are 4 sts on needle.

Next row K1, SK2P. Bind off rem 2 sts.

Side section 2

Next row (RS) Place sts on holder back to LH needle, join B, k 37 (41, 47), p1.

Next row K to last st, end p1. Change to A. Cont to work as for side section 1.

FINISHING

Place shawl over your shoulders. Bring back bottom corners under the arms and pin to bottom edge of front sections, forming armholes. Tack each corner securely in place.

TIE

Thread silk scarf in yarn needle. Beg at one front top corner, insert needle through top of color A st. Working across top edge, cont to insert needle through top of color A st every 2"/5cm to opposite front top corner.

BEADED LEAF
LACE SHAWL
Rhapsody in red

■■■■▶

Karen Joan Raz's ultra-femme, flame-stitch shawl is ablaze with fiery color and glittering gold glass beads. The spectacular lace-stitch pattern forms a striking mirror-image design.

SIZES

Instructions are written for one size.

FINISHED MEASUREMENTS

■ Width across top edge approx 86"/ 218.5cm

■ Length from neck to point approx 43"/ 109cm

MATERIALS

■ 2 2oz/60g balls (each approx 825yd/ 754m) of Jade Sapphire Exotic Fibres *Lacey Lamb* (extrafine lambswool) in #225 ruby (🔟)

■ Size 5 (3.75mm) circular needle, 24"/ 60cm long *or size to obtain gauge*

■ One size 6 (4mm) needle (for I-cord bind-off)

■ Steel crochet hook size 12 (1mm)

■ 900 size 6/0 silver-lined gold glass beads with A/B finish

■ Stitch markers

GAUGE

16 sts and 25 rows to 4"/10cm over chart pat 2 using size 5 (3.75mm) circular needle. *Take time to check gauge.*

Notes

1 The shawl is made from the top down and is composed of two identical sections that form a mirror image.

2 Only RS rows are shown on charts.

3 Chart 1, row 1, will inc 1 st per section (2 sts in total). Chart 1, row 27, and chart 2, row 23, will inc 4 sts per section (8 sts in total). All other charted rows will inc by 2 sts per section (4 sts in total).

STITCH GLOSSARY

Add bead Slide bead onto crochet hook. With hook in front, slip next st from LH needle onto hook. Slide bead onto st, then place st back on LH needle and knit.

SHAWL

With circular needle, cast on 6 sts. Knit next row.

Beg Chart 1

Row 1 (RS) K2, pm, work row 1 of chart 1 once, pm (for center of shawl), work row 1 of chart 1 once more—8 sts.

Row 2 and all WS rows K2, p to marker, sl marker, k2.

Row 3 K2, sl marker, work row 3 of chart 1 twice—12 sts.

Row 4 Rep row 2. Keeping 2 sts at beg of every RS row in garter st, cont to foll chart in this manner to row 27—64 sts.

Row 28 Rep row 2.

Beg Chart 2

First 24-row rep

Row 1 (RS) K2, slip marker, work row 1 of chart 2 twice—68 sts.

Row 2 and all WS rows K2, p to last 2 sts, end k2. Keeping 2 sts at beg of every RS row in garter st, cont to foll chart in this manner to row 23—116 sts.

Row 24 Rep row 2.

Second 24-row rep

Row 1 (RS) K2, slip marker, [work row 1 of chart 2 to first rep line, work 26-st rep twice, then work to end of chart row 1] twice—120 sts.

Row 2 and all WS rows K2, p to last 2 sts, end k2. Keeping 2 sts at beg of every RS row in garter st, cont to foll chart in this manner to row 23—168 sts.

Row 24 Rep row 2.

Third 24-row rep

Row 1 (RS) K2, slip marker, [work row 1 of chart 2 to first rep line, work 26-st rep 3 times, then work to end of chart row 1] twice—172 sts.

Row 2 and all WS rows K2, p to last 2 sts, end k2. Keeping 2 sts at beg of every RS row in garter st, cont to foll chart in this manner to row 23—220 sts.

Row 24 Rep row 2.

Fourth 24-row rep

Row 1 (RS) K2, slip marker, [work row 1 of chart 2 to first rep line, work 26-st rep 4 times, then work to end of chart row 1] twice—224 sts.

Row 2 and all WS rows K2, p to last 2 sts, end k2. Keeping 2 sts at beg of every RS row in garter st, cont to foll chart in this manner to row 23—272 sts.

Row 24 Rep row 2.

Fifth 24-row rep

Row 1 (RS) K2, slip marker, [work row 1 of chart 2 to first rep line, work 26-st rep 5 times, then work to end of chart row 1] twice—276 sts.

Row 2 and all WS rows K2, p to last 2 sts, end k2. Keeping 2 sts at beg of every RS row in garter st, cont to foll chart in this manner to row 23—324 sts.

Row 24 Rep row 2.

Sixth 24-row rep

Row 1 (RS) K2, slip marker, [work row 1 of chart 2 to first rep line, work 26-st rep 6 times, then work to end of chart row 1] twice—328 sts.

Row 2 and all WS rows K2, p to last 2 sts, end k2. Keeping 2 sts at beg of every RS row in garter st, cont to foll chart in this manner to row 23—376 sts.

Row 24 Rep row 2.

Seventh 24-row rep

Row 1 (RS) K2, slip marker, [work row 1 of chart 2 to first rep line, work 26-st rep 7

times, then work to end of chart row 1]
twice—380 sts.

Row 2 and all WS rows K2, p to last 2 sts,
end k2. Keeping 2 sts at beg of every RS
row in garter st, cont to foll chart in this
manner to row 23—428 sts.

Row 24 Rep row 2.

Eighth 24-row rep

Row 1 (RS) K2, slip marker, [work row 1
of chart 2 to first rep line, work 26-st rep 8
times, then work to end of chart row 1]
twice—432 sts.

Row 2 and all WS rows K2, p to last 2 sts,
end k2. Keeping 2 sts at beg of every RS
row in garter st, cont to foll chart in this
manner to row 23—480 sts.

Row 24 Rep row 2.

Beg Chart 3

Row 1 (RS) K2, slip marker, [work row 1
of chart 3 to first rep line, work 26-st rep 9
times, then work to end of chart row 1]
twice—484 sts.

Row 2 and all WS rows K2, p to last 2 sts,
end k2. Keeping 2 sts at beg of every RS
row in garter st, cont to foll chart in this
manner to row 21—524 sts.

Row 22 Rep row 2.

I-Cord bind-off

With RS facing and straight needle, *k1, ssk,
slip 2 sts on RH needle back to LH needle;
rep from * until 2 sts rem, end ssk, fasten off
last st.

Block piece to measurements.

Stitch Key

- ☐ K1
- O Yo
- ✕ K2tog
- ✕ SSK
- ⍺ K1-tbl
- **B** Add bead
- ⋏ SK2P
- ⋏ S2KP2

Chart 1

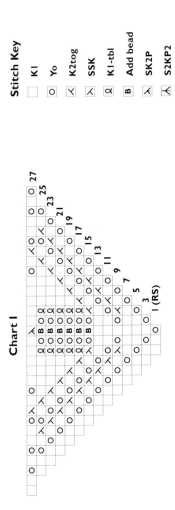

Chart 2

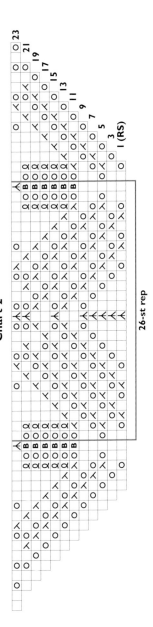

26-st rep

Chart 3

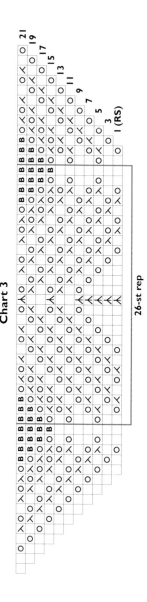

26-st rep

WAVE-PATTERN
SHAWL
In the limelight

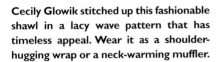

Cecily Glowik stitched up this fashionable shawl in a lacy wave pattern that has timeless appeal. Wear it as a shoulder-hugging wrap or a neck-warming muffler.

SIZES

Instructions are written for one size.

KNITTED MEASUREMENTS

■ Approx 14½"/37cm wide x 65"/165cm long

MATERIALS

■ 4 1¾oz/50g hanks (each approx 123yd/112m) of Classic Elite Yarns *Lush* (angora/wool) in #4481 granny smith (**4**)
■ One pair size 10 (6mm) needles *or size to obtain gauge*

GAUGE

17 sts and 22 rows to 4"/10cm over wave pat using size 10 (6mm) needles.
Take time to check gauge.

WAVE PATTERN

(multiple of 20 sts plus 2)

Row 1 (RS) P1, *p1, yo, k5, ssk, k4, k2tog, k5, yo, p1; rep from *, end p1.

Row 2 K1, *k1, p1, yo, p5, p2tog, p2, p2tog tbl, p5, yo, p1, k1; rep from *, end k1.

Row 3 P1, *p1, k2, yo, k5, ssk, k2tog, k5, yo, k2, p1; rep from*, end p1.

Row 4 K1, *k1, p3, yo, p1, p2tog, p6, p2tog tbl, p1, yo, p3, k1; rep from*, end k1.

Rep rows 1–4 for wave pat.

SHAWL

Cast on 62 sts. Knit next row. Cont in wave pat until piece measures approx 65"/165cm from beg, end with row 3. Knit next row. Bind off all sts loosely knitwise.

FINISHING

Block piece lightly to measurements.

Wave Pattern Chart

20-st rep

Stitch Key

☐ K on RS, P on WS

⊟ P on RS, K on WS

⊙ Yo

◣ K2tog on RS, p2tog on WS

◢ SSK on RS, p2tog-tbl on WS

■■■□

Valentina Devine's shawl of bright color blocks bordered by strips of black was inspired by the bold geometric paintings of the Modern Art movement. Because you join each strip of blocks to the previous one as you knit, no sewing is necessary.

SIZES

Instructions are written for one size.

KNITTED MEASUREMENTS

■ Approx 72"/183cm wide x 25"/63.5cm long *(excluding fringe)*

MATERIALS

■ 7 1.4oz/40g balls (each approx 89yd/ 81m) of Ironstone Yarns *Brushed Mohair* (mohair/wool/nylon) in #100 black (MC)

■ One ball each in #309 lavender (A), #205 hollyhock (B), #728 olive (C), #211 blue (D), #411 gold (E), #492 fuchsia (F), #210 viola (G), #306 light blue (H), #402 orange (I), #701 forest green (J), #490 red (K) and #703 turquoise (L) 🔁

■ One pair size 10 (6mm) needles *or size to obtain gauge*

■ Size I/9 (5.5mm) crochet hook

GAUGE

14¼ sts and 25 1/2 rows to 4"/10cm over garter st using size 10 (6mm) needles. *Take time to check gauge.*

STRIP I

With A, cast on 13 sts.

Rows 1–22 K1 tbl, k to last st, sl last st purlwise. Change to B.

Rows 23–44 Rep row 1. Change to MC.

Rows 45–66 Rep row 1. Change to C.

Rows 67–88 Rep row 1. Change to D.

Rows 89–110 Rep row 1. Change to MC.

Rows 111–132 Rep row 1. Change to E.

Rows 133–154 Rep row 1. Bind off.

STRIP 2

With MC, cast on 13 sts.

Joining

Row 1 (RS) K 1 tbl, k to last st, sl last st, insert LH needle into first st of row 1 of strip 1, sl st on RH needle onto LH needle and k the 2 sts tog.

Row 2 With MC, k 1 tbl, k to last st, sl last st purlwise.

Row 3 K1 tbl, k to last st, sl last st, insert LH needle into first st of row 3 of strip 1, sl st on RH needle onto LH needle and k the 2 sts tog.

Row 4 Rep row 2.

Row 5 K1 tbl, k to last st, sl last st, insert LH needle into first st of row 5 of strip 1, sl st on RH needle onto LH needle and k the 2 sts tog.

Row 6 Rep row 2.

Cont in this manner, joining strip 2 to strip 1 every RS row until 154 rows of MC have been completed and strips are joined. Bind off.

With F, cast on 13 sts.

Joining

Row 1 (RS) K1 tbl, k to last st, sl last st, insert LH needle into first st of row 1 of strip 2, sl st on RH needle onto LH needle and k the 2 sts tog.

Row 2 K1 tbl, k to last st, sl last st purlwise.

Row 3 K1 tbl, k to last st, sl last st, insert LH needle into first st of row 3 of strip 2, sl st on RH needle onto LH needle and k the 2 sts tog.

Row 4 Rep row 2.

Row 5 K1 tbl, k to last st, sl last st, insert LH needle into first st of row 5 of strip 2, sl st on RH needle onto LH needle and k the 2 sts tog.

Row 6 Rep row 2.

Cont in this manner, joining strip 3 to strip 2 every RS row until 22 rows of F have been completed. Refer to color placement diagram and cont to work color block pat and joining strips tog as established.

STRIPS 4–21

Refer to color placement diagram and cont to work and join strips tog, working 22 rows for each of the 7-block strips and 154 rows for each MC strip.

EDGING

With RS facing and crochet hook, join MC with a sl st in top right corner.

Rnd 1 (RS) Ch 1, sc in same place as joining, making sure that work lies flat, sc evenly around entire edge, working 3 sc in each corner, join rnd with a sl st in first sc.

Rnd 2 Ch 1, sc in each st across top edge to opposite top corner, *ch 3, sk next 2 sts, sc in next 2 sts; rep from * around rem 3 sides, join rnd with a sl st in first st. Fasten off.

FRINGE

Cut 12"/30.5cm strands of MC. Using 4 strands for each fringe, attach a fringe in each ch-3 sp along edging. Trim ends evenly.

Color Placement Diagram

D	MC	E	G	MC	C	F
			MC			
B	MC	L	H	MC	G	A
C	MC	F	I	MC	J	B
			MC			
B	MC	G	C	MC	E	L
J	MC	A	K	MC	H	F
			MC			
H	MC	E	B	MC	L	A
K	MC	J	H	MC	C	I
			MC			
A	MC	F	E	MC	K	J
B	MC	C	G	MC	H	B
			MC			
J	MC	E	L	MC	F	C
I	MC	D	B	MC	L	H
			MC			
F	MC	C	K	MC	E	J
J	MC	I	H	MC	G	F
			MC			
E	MC	D	C	MC	B	A

COLOR KEY

(MC) Black
(A) Lavender
(B) Hollyhock
(C) Olive
(D) Blue
(E) Gold
(F) Fuchsia
(G) Viola
(H) Light blue
(I) Orange
(J) Forest green
(K) Red
(L) Turquoise

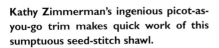

Kathy Zimmerman's ingenious picot-as-you-go trim makes quick work of this sumptuous seed-stitch shawl.

SIZES
Instructions are written for one size.

KNITTED MEASUREMENTS
■ Width across top edge approx 76"/193cm
■ Length from neck to point approx 35"/89cm

MATERIALS
■ 8 2¾oz/78g hanks (each approx 100yd/91m) of Kolláge Yarns *Illumination* (mohair/viscose/polyamide blend) in silent tide (**4**)
■ One pair size 11 (8mm) needles *or size to obtain gauge*

GAUGE
11 sts and 19¾ rows to 4"/10cm over seed st using size 11 (8mm) needles.
Take time to check gauge.

Notes
1 Shawl is made vertically from top corner to top corner.
2 Picot edging is added as you work by casting on and binding off sts.
3 Use knit-on method (see page 15) for casting on.

SEED STITCH
All rows Knit the p sts and purl the k sts.

SHAWL
First Half
Note To inc 1 st in seed st, p into front and back of st if st is to be purled, *or* k into front and back of st if st is to be knitted.
Cast on 2 sts.
Row 1 (WS) K1, p1.
Row 2 (RS) Cast-on 3 sts, bind off 3 sts, k1.
Row 3 K1, inc 1 st in next st.
Row 4 Cast-on 3 sts, bind off 3 sts, work in seed st to end.
Row 5 Work in seed st to last st, inc 1 st in last st.
Rep rows 4 and 5 until there are 95 sts on needle *(not including 3 cast-on sts)*, end with a WS row. Piece should measure approx 38"/96.5cm from beg.
Second Half
Note To dec 1 st in seed st, p2tog if next to last st is to be purled or k2tog if next to last st is to be knitted.
Next row (RS) Cast on 3 sts, bind off 3 sts, work in seed st to end.
Next row Work in seed st to last 2 sts, work next 2 sts tog.
Rep these 2 rows until 2 sts rem. Bind off in seed st.

FINISHING
Block piece lightly to measurements.

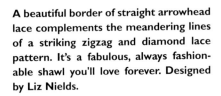

A beautiful border of straight arrowhead lace complements the meandering lines of a striking zigzag and diamond lace pattern. It's a fabulous, always fashionable shawl you'll love forever. Designed by Liz Nields.

SIZES

Instructions are written for one size.

KNITTED MEASUREMENTS

■ Approx 22"/56cm wide x 66"/167.5cm long

MATERIALS

■ 7 .88oz/25g skeins (each approx 171yd/156m) of Naturally NZ/Fiber Trends *Dawn* (wool/silk) in #3 rust ■
■ One pair size 5 (3.75mm) needles *or size to obtain gauge*
■ Size 5 (3.75mm) circular needle, 24"/60cm long *or size to obtain gauge*
■ Size D/3 (3.25mm) crochet hook
■ Contrasting sport weight yarn (waste yarn)
■ Stitch markers (one a different color)

GAUGE

27¾ sts to 5¼"/13.5cm and 32¼ rows to 4"/10cm over chart 1 using size 5 (3.75mm) needles *(after blocking)*.
14¼ sts to 3"/7.5cm and 20 rows to 2"/5cm over border pat rib using size 5 (3.75mm) circular needle (after blocking).
Take time to check gauges.

SHAWL

With crochet hook and waste yarn, ch 102. Cut yarn and draw end though lp on hook. Turn ch so bottom lps are at top and cut end is at LH side. With straight needles, beg 2 lps from opposite end, pick up and k 1 st in each of next 95 lps. Purl one row.

Beg chart I

Row I (RS) Beg with st 1 and work to st 47, rep sts 18–47 once, then work sts 48 to 65. Cont to foll chart in this manner to row 20, then rep rows 1–20 24 times more. Place sts on a length of waste yarn.

FINISHING

Block piece to measurements.

BORDER

Place sts on length of waste yarn back to LH needle ready for a RS row.

Prep rnd With circular needle, knit, dec 9 sts evenly spaced across sts on needle, (pm, yo, pm) for 1st corner, pick up and k 247 sts along side edge, (pm, yo, pm) for 2nd corner, with RS facing, release cut end from lp of waste yarn ch at beg edge, pull out 1 ch at a time, placing sts on LH needle, then knit dec 9 sts evenly spaced across sts on needle, (pm, yo, pm) for 3rd corner, pick up and k 247 sts along side, (pm, yo, pm of different color to indicate beg of rnd) for last corner—670 sts.

Next rnd Purl.

Rnd I [*P2, yo, ssk, k1, k2tog, yo; rep from

* to 2 sts before marker, p2, sl marker, work row 3 of chart 2, sl marker] 4 times.

Rnd 2 [*P2, k5; rep from * to 2 sts before marker, p2, sl marker, work row 4 of chart 2, sl marker] 4 times.

Rnd 3 [*P2, k1, yo, SK2P, yo, k1; rep from * to 2 sts before marker, p2, sl marker, work row 5 of chart 2, sl marker] 4 times.

Rnd 4 [*P2, k5; rep from * to 2 sts before marker, p2, sl marker, work row 6 of chart 2, sl marker] 4 times.

Rnd 5 Rep rnd 1, working row 7 of chart 2 bet markers at corners.

Rnd 6 Rep rnd 2, working row 8 of chart 2 bet markers at corners.

Rnd 7 Rep rnd 3, working row 9 of chart 2 bet markers at corners

Rnd 8 Rep rnd 4, working row 10 of chart 2 bet markers at corners.

Rep rnds 1–4 twice more, then rnds 1–3 once, AT THE SAME TIME, cont to work chart 2 rows 11–21 as established.

Bind off as foll: with WS facing and crochet hook, [insert hook into next st on needle, yo and draw up a lp, slip st off needle and onto hook] twice, yo and draw through 2 lps on hook,*insert hook into next st on needle, yo and draw up a lp, slip st off needle and onto hook, yo and draw through 2 lps on hook; rep from * to end. Cut yarn, fasten off last st.

Chart I

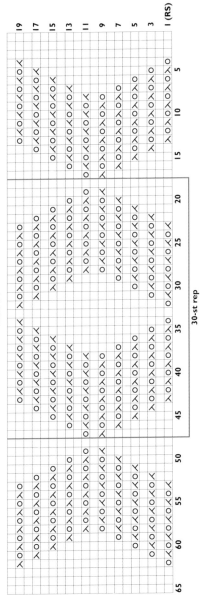

Chart 2

Stitch Key

	K on RS, P on WS
	P on RS, K on WS
O	Yo
⅄	SSK
⅃	K2tog
⅄	SK2P

DOUBLE
DIAMOND SHAWL
Scarborough fair

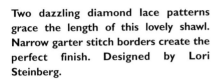

Two dazzling diamond lace patterns grace the length of this lovely shawl. Narrow garter stitch borders create the perfect finish. Designed by Lori Steinberg.

SIZES

Instructions are written for one size.

KNITTED MEASUREMENTS

■ Approx 24"/61cm wide x 62"/157.5cm long

MATERIALS

■ 5 1¾oz/50g skeins (each approx 137yd/125m) of Knit One, Crochet Too, Inc. *Ambrosia* (baby alpaca/silk/cashmere) in #729 lavender mist (MC) ⬛

■ 2 skeins in #510 pale moss (CC)

■ One pair size 6 (4mm) needles *or size to obtain gauge*

■ Size 6 (4mm) circular needle, 24"/60cm long

■ Size G/6 (4mm) crochet hook

■ Contrasting sport weight yarn (waste yarn)

GAUGE

18 sts and 26 rows to 4"/10cm over St st using size 6 (4mm) straight needles. *Take time to check gauge.*

Notes

1 Only RS rows are shown on charts.
2 Purl all WS rows.

SHAWL

With crochet hook and waste yarn, ch 105. Cut yarn and draw end though lp on hook. Turn ch so bottom lps are at top and cut end is at LH side. With straight needles and MC, beg 2 lps from RH end of ch, pick up and k 1 st in each of next 98 lps. Knit one row. Purl one row.

Beg chart 1

Row 1 (RS) Beg with st 1 and work to st 17, rep sts 2–17 4 times, then work sts 18 to 34. Cont to foll chart in this manner to row 32, then rep rows 1–32 5 times more, then rows 1–22 once. Cont as foll:

Rows 1 and 2 With MC, purl.
Rows 3 and 4 With CC, knit.
Rows 5 and 6 With MC, knit.
Rows 7 and 8 With CC, knit.
Row 9 With MC, knit.
Rows 10–12 With MC, purl.

Beg chart 2

Row 1 (RS) Beg with st 1 and work to st 23, rep sts 6–23 3 times, then work sts 24 to 44. Cont to foll chart in this manner to row 38. Change to CC and rep rows 3–38. Cont as foll:

Next 3 rows Purl. Bind off all sts knitwise.

Opposite side

Release cut end from lp of waste yarn ch. Pull out 1 ch at a time, placing each st on LH needle ready for a WS row. Cont as foll:

Row 1 (WS) With MC, purl.
Rows 2 and 3 With CC, knit.
Rows 4 and 5 With MC, knit.

Rows 6 and 7 With CC, knit.

Row 8 With MC, purl.

Rows 9–11 With MC, purl.

Beg chart 2

Row 1 (RS) Beg with st 1 and work to st 23, rep sts 6–23 3 times, then work sts 24 to 44. Cont to foll chart in this manner to row 38. Change to CC and rep rows 3–38. Cont as foll:

Next 3 rows Purl. Bind off all sts knitwise.

With RS facing, circular needle and CC, pick up and k 256 sts evenly spaced across one long side edge. Knit next 4 rows. Bind off all sts loosely knitwise. Rep for opposite long side edge.

Block piece to measurements.

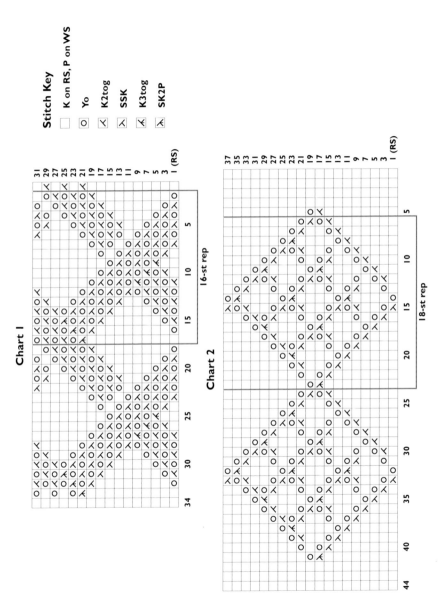

Stitch Key

☐	K on RS, P on WS
O	Yo
⊼	K2tog
⋏	SSK
⊼	K3tog
⋏	SK2P

Chart I

16-st rep

Chart 2

18-st rep

51

■■■ ▭

Liz Nields puts a whole new spin on a "shawl collar" with her cropped ruffled wrap that ties at the neck. Wear it over bare shoulders or layer on top of a turtleneck.

SIZES

Instructions are written for one size.

KNITTED MEASUREMENTS

■ Width across bottom edge approx 45"/ 114.5cm

■ Length from neck to bottom edge 9"/ 23cm

MATERIALS

■ 2 4oz/113g hanks (each approx 330yd/ 302m) of The Schaefer Yarn Company *Judith* (prime alpaca) in Gertrude Ederle **③**

■ Size 5 (3.75mm) circular needle, 40"/100cm long *or size to obtain gauge*

■ Two size 5 (3.75mm) dpns (for I-cord tie)

GAUGE

22 sts and 26 rows to 4"/10cm over St st using size 5 (3.75mm) circular needle. *Take time to check gauge.*

Note

Ruffles are added after knitting is completed.

CAPELET

With circular needle, cast on 240 sts. Do *not* join.

Working back and forth, knit next 2 rows.

Inc row 1 (WS) K12, *M1, k26; rep from * 7 times more, end M1, k11—249 sts. Cont as foll:

Next row (RS) Sl 1 wyif, k to end.

Next row Sl 1 wyif, k2, p to last 3 sts, end k3.

Rep last 2 rows until piece measures 3¾"/9.5cm from beg, end with a WS row.

Dec row 2 (RS) Sl 1 wyif, k8, *SK2P, k9; rep from * to last 12 sts, end SK2P, k9—209 sts.

Next row Sl 1 wyif, k2, p to last 3 sts, end k3.

Dec row 3 (RS) Sl 1 wyif, *k17, SK2P*; rep from * to * twice more, k87, **SK2P, k17**; rep from ** to ** twice more, end k1—197 sts.

Next row Knit—*for center ruffle garter st ridge.*

Tuck

Row 1 (RS) Sl 1 wyif, k to end.

Row 2 Sl 1 wyif, k2, p to last 3 sts, end k3. Rep these 2 rows twice more.

Next (tuck) row (RS) Sl first st knitwise onto RH needle, on WS, insert tip of RH needle in top of first p-st of 6 rows below, sl both sts to LH needle, then k them both tog, *sl next st knitwise onto RH needle, on WS, insert tip of RH needle in top of next p-st of 6 rows below. Sl both sts to LH needle, then k them both tog; rep from * to end.

Next row Sl 1 wyif, k to end. Rep rows 1 and 2 once more.

Dec row 4 (RS) Sl 1 wyif, k15, *SK2P, k15; rep from * to end—177 sts.

Rep row 2 once, then rows 1 and 2 3 times.

Dec row 5 (RS) Sl 1 wyif, k14, *SK2P, k13; rep from *, end k1—157 sts.

Rep row 2 once, then rows 1 and 2 3 times.

Dec row 6 (RS) Sl 1 wyif, k13, *SK2P, k11; rep from *, end k2—137 sts.

Rep row 2 once, then rows 1 and 2 3 times.

Dec row 7 (RS) Sl 1 wyif, k12, *SK2P, k9; rep from *, end k3—117 sts.

Next row Knit—*for top ruffle garter st ridge.*

Drawstring casing

Rows 1 and 3 Knit.

Row 2 Purl.

Row 4 Knit for garter st turning ridge.

Rows 5 and 7 Knit.

Rows 6 and 8 Purl. Bind off.

BOTTOM RUFFLE

With RS facing and circular needle, skip first st, pick up and k 1 st in each of next 238 sts, leaving last st unworked.

Next row (WS) Knit.

Next (inc) row (RS) Knit in front and back of each st to end—476 sts.

Next row Knit.

Next (inc) row (RS) Knit in front and back of each st to end—952 sts.

Next row Knit. Bind off all sts knitwise.

CENTER RUFFLE

With RS facing, bottom edge at top and circular needle, skip first st of center ruffle garter st ridge, pick up and k 1 st in each of next 195 sts, leaving last st unworked.

Next row (WS) Knit.

Next (inc) row (RS) Knit in front, back and front of each st to end—585 sts.

Next row Knit.

Bind off all sts knitwise.

TOP RUFFLE

With RS facing, bottom edge at top and circular needle, skip first st of top ruffle garter st ridge, pick up and k 1 st in each of next 115 sts, leaving last st unworked.

Next row (WS) Knit.

Next (inc) row (RS) Knit in front, back and front of each st to end—345 sts.

Next row Knit.

Bind off all sts knitwise.

FINISHING

Fold drawstring casing to WS along garter st turning ridge and sew in place.

DRAWSTRING

With dpn, cast on 3 sts. Work in I-cord as foll:

*Next row (RS) With 2nd dpn, k3, *do not turn.* Slide sts back to beg of needle to work next row from RS; rep from * until piece measures 52"/132cm from beg.

Cut yarn leaving a long tail. Thread tail into tapestry needle, then weave needle through sts; fasten off securely. Thread drawstring through casing.

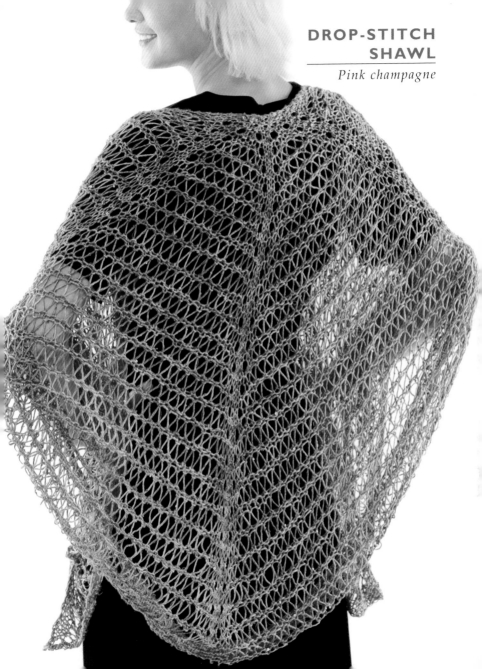

This spectacular semicircular shawl is knit using a satiny spun-silk yarn dotted with tiny glittering sequins. The dramatic drop-stitch pattern gives it its light and airy look. Designed by Debbie O'Neill.

SIZES

Instructions are written for one size.

KNITTED MEASUREMENTS

■ Width across top edge approx 72"/ 183cm

■ Length from neck to bottom edge 36"/ 91.5cm

MATERIALS

■ 3 3½oz/100g hanks (each approx 225yd/206m) of Tilli Tomas *Disco Lights* (spun silk/petite sequins) in hibiscus 🔳

■ Size 10 (6mm) circular needle, 40"/ 101cm long *or size to obtain gauge*

■ Stitch markers

GAUGE

8¼ sts to 4"/10cm over drop st pat using size 10 (6mm) circular needle.
Take time to check gauge.

Notes

1 Shawl is made in one piece from the top down.

2 Shawl is divided into four triangular sections that form the half-circle shape.

SHAWL

Cast on 4 sts.

Row 1 (inc) K into front and back of each st across—8 sts.

Row 2 [K2, pm] 3 times, k2. *Markers indicate four sections: two side sections and two center sections.*

Rows 3 and 4 Knit.

Row 5 (inc) K into front and back of each st across—16 sts.

Row 6 Knit.

Row 7 (inc) K into front and back of first st, k to last st, k into front and back of last st—18 sts. *From this point forward, each of the two side sections will have 1 more st than the two center sections.*

Row 8 Knit.

Row 9 (inc) K1, *k1, yo, k2, yo, k1; rep from * to last st, end k1—26 sts *(7 sts in each side panel and 6 sts in each center panel).*

Row 10 Knit.

Row 11 K1, *k2, [k1, yo] twice, k2; rep from * to last st, end k1.

Row 12 Knit across, dropping extra wraps.

Row 13 (inc) K1, *k1, yo, k to 1 st before marker, yo, k1; rep from * to last st, end k1—34 sts.

Row 14 Knit.

Row 15 K1, [k2, *k1, yo twice; rep from * to 2 sts before marker, k2] 3 times, k2, rep from * to * to last 3 sts, end k3.

Row 16 Knit across, dropping extra wraps.

Rep rows 13–16 23 times more—218 sts *(55 sts in each side panel and 54 sts in each center panel)*.

Row 109 Rep row 13—226 sts.

Rows 110—112 Knit.

Row 113 Rep row 13—234 sts.

Rows 114—116 Knit. Bind off last row as foll: using a slightly looser tension, k first 2 sts. Sl these sts, one st at a time, back to LH needle, k these 2 sts tog, *k next st, sl 2 sts on RH needle, one st at a time, back to LH needle, k these 2 sts tog; rep from * until 1 st rem. Fasten off last st.

FINISHING

Block piece lightly to measurements.

■■■◻

Cecily Glowik has accented her lovely cashmere shawl with elegant I-cord looped edging that's an inventive alternative to classic fringe trim.

SIZES
Instructions are written for one size.

KNITTED MEASUREMENTS
■ Approx 15½"/39cm wide x 65"/165cm long *(excluding edging)*

MATERIALS
■ 6 1¾oz/50g balls (each approx 125yd/114m) of Classic Elite Yarns *Lavish* (cashmere) in #10187 grey (❹)
■ Size 10 (6mm) needles *or size to obtain gauge*
■ Two size 10 (6mm) dpns (for I-cord edging)

GAUGE
15 sts and 22 rows to 4"/10cm over diamond scallop st using size 10 (6mm) needles. *Take time to check gauge.*

DIAMOND SCALLOP STITCH
(multiple of 8 sts plus 2)
Rows I and 3 (WS) Purl.
Row 2 K1, *wyib, insert RH needle under running thread between st just worked and next st and place on needle, k2, pass running thread over the 2 knit sts, k2; rep from *, end k1.

Row 4 K3, *wyib, insert RH needle under running thread between st just worked and next st and place on needle, k2, pass running thread over the 2 knit sts, k2; rep from *, end last rep k1.
Rep rows 1–4 for diamond scallop st.

WRAP
With straight needles, cast on 58 sts. Work in diamond scallop st until piece measures 65"/165cm from beg, end with a WS row. Bind off.

I-CORDS (make 2)
With dpn, cast on 4 sts. Work in I-cord as foll:
*Next row (RS) With 2nd dpn, k4, *do not turn.* Slide sts back to beg of needle to work next row from RS; rep from * until piece measures 41"/104cm from beg. Cut yarn, leaving a long tail. Thread tail into tapestry needle, then weave needle through sts; fasten off securely.

FINISHING
Block piece to measurements.

LOOPED EDGING
With RS facing, pin an I-cord to bound-off edge, forming five 1½"/4cm diameter loops that are spaced approx 1¾"/4.5cm apart and making sure the 3rd loop is centered. Sew in place. Rep for cast-on edge.

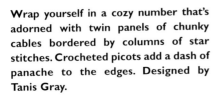

Wrap yourself in a cozy number that's adorned with twin panels of chunky cables bordered by columns of star stitches. Crocheted picots add a dash of panache to the edges. Designed by Tanis Gray.

SIZES
Instructions are written for one size.

KNITTED MEASUREMENTS
- Approx 23½"/59.5cm wide x 55½"/141cm long *(excluding edging)*

MATERIALS
- 15 1¾oz/50g hanks *(each approx 86yd/79m)* of Alchemy Yarns of Transformation *Wabi Sabi* (silk/wool) in #21e green plum (5)
- One pair size 9 (5.5mm) needles *or size to obtain gauge*
- Cable needle
- Size I/9 (5.5mm) crochet hook

GAUGE
16 sts and 22 rows to 4"/10cm over St st using size 9 (5.5mm) needles.
Take time to check gauge.

STITCH GLOSSARY
MS (make star) P3tog leaving sts on needle, yo, then p the same 3 sts tog again.

4-st RC Sl 2 sts to cn and hold in *back*, k2, k2 from cn.

4-st LC Sl 2 sts to cn and hold in *front*, k2, k2 from cn.

3-st RPC Sl next st to cn and hold in *back*, k2, p1 from cn.

3-st LPC Sl 2 sts to cn and hold in *front*, p1, k2 from cn.

WRAP
Cast on 119 sts.
Beg chart
Row 1 (RS) Beg with st 1 and work to st 68, then work sts 20 to 70. Cont to foll chart in this manner to row 24, then rep rows 1–24 11 times more. Bind off.

FINISHING
Block lightly to measurements.

EDGING
With RS facing and crochet hook, join yarn with a sl st in any corner.
Rnd 1 (RS) Ch 1, sc in same place as joining, making sure that work lies flat, work 3 sc evenly spaced, *ch 3, sl st in 3rd ch from hook *(picot made)*, *work 4 sc evenly spaced, make picot; rep from * around, join rnd with a sl st in first sc. Fasten off.

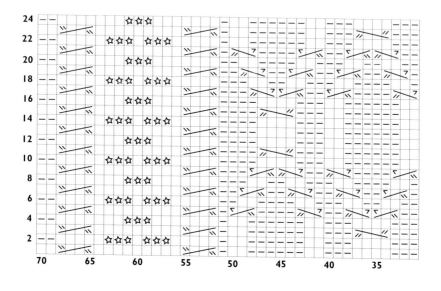

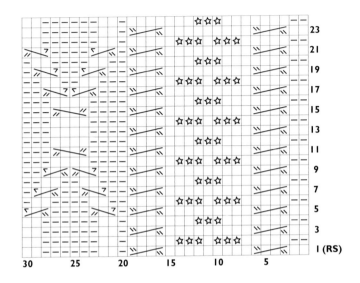

Stitch Key

☐	**K on RS, P on WS**
−	**P on RS, K on WS**
⊻	**3-st RPC**
⊼	**3-st LPC**
⊻	**4-st RC**
⊼	**4-st LC**
☆☆☆	**MS**

TEXTURED ZIGZAG
SHAWL

Catch some zzz's

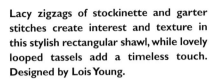

Lacy zigzags of stockinette and garter stitches create interest and texture in this stylish rectangular shawl, while lovely looped tassels add a timeless touch. Designed by Lois Young.

SIZES

Instructions are written for one size.

KNITTED MEASUREMENTS

■ Approx 20½"/52cm wide x 63"/160cm long *(excluding tassels)*

MATERIALS

■ 7 1¾oz/50g skeins (each approx 120yd/110m) of Dale of Norway *Harlequin* (wool/microfiber/alpaca/cashmere/viscose) in #10 mauve ■

■ One pair size 8 (5mm) needles *or size to obtain gauge*

GAUGE

15½ sts and 22¼ rows to 4"/10cm over chart pat using size 8 (5mm) needles *(after blocking).*
Take time to check gauge.

SHAWL

Cast on 79 sts loosely.
Next row (RS) Knit.
Next row K3, p73, k3.
Beg chart
Row 1 (RS) Beg with st 1 and work to st 25, rep sts 14–25 4 times, then work sts 26 to 31. Cont to foll chart in this manner to row 16, then rep rows 1–16 21 times more, end with a WS row.
Next row (RS) Knit.
Next row K3, p73, k3. Bind off all sts knitwise.

FINISHING

Block piece to measurements.

TASSELS (MAKE 14)

Leaving a 8"/20.5cm tail, cast on 7 sts loosely. Knit next 10 rows. Bind off 2 sts (tassel top). Cut yarn, leaving a 10"/25.5cm tail, then draw through st on RH needle to fasten off. Remove rem 4 sts from LH needle, then unravel them to form 6 loops. Thread long tail in tapestry needle. Roll top of tassel tightly towards longer tail. Use this tail to sew the side edge of the roll to secure it in place, then use same tail to wrap 4 times around base of tassel top. Make a few sts to secure wraps, then insert needle up through center of tassel top so needle exits center top. Remove needle. Trim shorter tail even with bottom of loops. Using longer tails to sew tassels to cast-on and bound-off edges, sew one to each corner, then one centered beneath each St st zigzag.

Zigzag Lace Pattern Chart

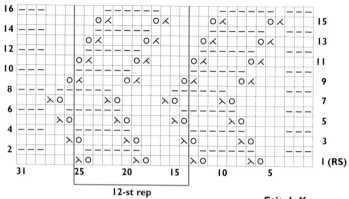

12-st rep

Stitch Key

☐	K on RS, P on WS
⊟	P on RS, K on WS
O	Yo
⋌	K2tog
⋋	SSK

Variegated yarn offers a pattern of end-
less color changes without all the bother.
It's a perfect pick for Amy Polcyn's smart
stockinette-stitch shawl trimmed with
bands of garter stitch.

SIZES

Instructions are written for one size.

KNITTED MEASUREMENTS

■ Width across top edge approx 62"/
157.5cm
■ Length from neck to bottom edge
26"/66cm

MATERIALS

■ 5 3½oz/100g hanks (each approx
215yd/197m) of Malabrigo Yarns *Worsted*
(merino wool) in #224 autumn forest (4)
■ One pair size 10 (6mm) needles *or size
to obtain gauge*
■ Size H/8 (5mm) crochet hook
■ Contrasting worsted weight yarn (waste
yarn)

GAUGE

16 sts and 22 rows to 4"/10cm over St st
using size 10 (6mm) needles.
Take time to check gauge.

Notes
1 Back section of shawl is worked vertically
from side to side using short-row wrapping.
2 Each front section is worked out from the
back section.

SHORT-ROW WRAPPING
(wrap and turn—w&t)
1 On knit side, wyib, sl next st purlwise.
2 Move yarn between the needles to the
front.
3 Sl the same st back to LH needle. Turn
work, bring yarn to the purl side between
the needles—*one st wrapped.*
4 When short rows are completed, work to
just before the wrapped st. Insert RH needle
under the wrap knitwise and knit it tog with
next stitch on LH needle.

SHAWL
Back section
With crochet hook and waste yarn, ch 102.
Cut yarn and draw end though lp on hook.
Turn ch so bottom lps are at top and cut end
is at LH side. With needles, beg 2 lps from
opposite end, pick up and k 1 st in each of
next 95 lps. Purl next row.
Short rows
Set-up row (WS) K5, p to last 5 sts, end
k5.
Row 1 (RS) K 84, w&t.
Row 2 and all WS rows K5, p to last 5 sts,
end k5.
Row 3 K67, w&t.
Row 5 K50, w&t.
Row 7 K33, w&t.
Row 9 K16, w&t.
Row 11 Knit across, picking up wraps and
knitting them tog with next st.
Rows 13, 15, 17 and 19 Knit.

Rows 14, 16, 18, and 20 Rep row 2.

Rep rows 1–20 9 times more, then rep row 1–12 once more.

Right front section

Dec row 1 (RS) K5, ssk, k to end.

Next row K5, p to last 5 sts, end k5. Rep last 2 rows 29 times more—65 sts.

Dec row 2 (RS) K5, ssk, k to end.

Dec row 3 K5, p to last 7 sts, end p2tog, k5.

Rep last 2 rows 26 times more, then dec row 1 once more—10 sts.

Work even in garter st on all sts for 1"/2.5cm. Bind off.

Left front section

With RS facing, release cut end from lp of waste yarn ch. Pulling out 1 ch at a time, place sts from back section on LH needle ready for a RS row.

Dec row 1 (RS) K to last 7 sts, end k2tog, k5.

Next row K5, p to last 5 sts, end k5. Rep last 2 rows 29 times more—65 sts.

Dec row 2 (RS) K to last 7 sts, end k2tog, k5.

Dec row 3 K5, p2tog tbl, p to last 5 sts, end k5.

Rep last 2 rows 26 times more, then dec row 1 once more—10 sts.

Work even in garter st on all sts for 1"/2.5cm. Bind off.

FINISHING

Block piece to measurements.

Put on the glitz for an evening out with this golden tri-corner garter-stitch shawl. Designed by Margery Winter.

SIZES

Instructions are written for one size.

KNITTED MEASUREMENTS

■ Width across top edge approx 46"/117cm
■ Length from top edge to point approx 26"/66cm

MATERIALS

■ 6 .88oz/25g hanks (each approx 95yd/87m) of Berroco, Inc., *Lumina* (cotton/acrylic/polyester) in #1620 gold coast (MC) ▣
■ 1 1¾oz/50g hank (each approx 144yd/133m) of Berroco, Inc., *Ultra Alpaca Light* (super fine alpaca/Peruvian wool) in #4205 dark chocolate (CC) ▣
■ Size 10 (6mm) circular needle, 24"/60cm long *or size to obtain gauge*
■ Size F/5 (3.75mm) crochet hook

GAUGE

12½ sts and 22 rows to 4"/10cm over garter st using size 10 (6mm) circular needle. *Take time to check gauge.*

SHAWL

With MC, cast on 2 sts.
Row 1 (RS) K1, M1, k1—3 sts.
Row 2 K1, M1, k2—4 sts.
Row 3 K1, M1, k3—5 sts.
Row 4 K1, M1, k to end—6 sts.
Rep row 4 until there are 145 sts on needle.
Bind off all sts loosely knitwise.

EDGING

With RS facing and crochet hook, join CC with a sl st in first bound-off st of top edge.
Rnd 1 (RS) Ch 1, sc in same st a joining, cont to sc in each bound-off st across, turn to side edge; making sure that work lies flat work: *ch 3, sc in side edge*; rep from * to * 57 times more to before bottom point, work (sc, ch 1, sc) in point, ch 3, then rep from * to * 58 times to before top edge, ch 3, join rnd with a sl st in first sc.
Rnd 2 Ch 1, sc in same st as joining, *ch 2, skip next 2 sts, sc in next st; rep from * across top edge, turn to side edge, work 5 dc in next ch-3 sp, **ch 1, skip next ch-3 sp, work 5 dc in next ch-3 sp**; rep from ** to ** to bottom ch-1 sp, work 5 dc in ch-1 sp, work 5 dc in next ch-3 sp; rep from ** to ** to top edge, join rnd with a sl st in first sc. Fasten off.

TANGO SHAWL
Red hot

Spice up your wardrobe options with a stylish shawl that you wear like a vest. Designed by Norah Gaughan.

SIZES
Instructions are written for Small/Medium. Changes for Large/X-Large are in parentheses.

KNITTED MEASUREMENTS
- Width 54 (62)"/127 (157.5)cm
- Length 27 (29)"/68.5 (73.5)cm

MATERIALS
- 11 (14) 1.4oz/40g hanks (each approx 100yd/91m) of Berroco, Inc., *Seduce* (rayon/linen/silk/nylon) in #4445 cinnabar lacquer (4)
- Size 8 (5mm) circular needle, 24"/60cm long *or size to obtain gauge*

GAUGE
24 sts to 5"/12.5cm and 26 rows to 4"/10cm over pat st using size 8 (5mm) circular needle. *Take time to check gauge.*

PATTERN STITCH
(multiple of 7 sts plus 2)
Row 1 (RS) K2, *k2tog, yo, k1, yo, ssk, k2; rep from * to end.
Row 2 K2, *p5, k2; rep from * to end.
Rep rows 1 and 2 for pat st.

BACK AND FRONTS
Beg at bottom edge, cast on 261 (296) sts. Do *not* join. Work back and forth in pat st until piece measures 14 (15)"/35.5 (38)cm from beg, end with a WS row.
Divide for armholes
Next row (RS) Work across first 92 (106) sts, join a second ball of yarn and work across center 77 (84) sts, join a third ball of yarn and work across last 92 (106) sts. Working each section separately, work even until armhole measures 8 (9)"/20.5 (23)cm, end with a WS row.
Next (joining) row (RS) With first ball of yarn, work across all sts dropping second and third balls—261 (296) sts. Cont to work even until piece measures 27 (29)"/68.5 (73.5)cm from beg, end with a WS row. Bind off all sts loosely.

FINISHING
Block piece to measurements.

Designer Barry Klein has partnered silky ribbon and gold-flecked mohair yarns to fashion a generously sized wrap that's rich in texture.

SIZES

Instructions are written for one size.

KNITTED MEASUREMENTS

■ Approx 23"/58.5cm wide x 64"/162.5cm long

MATERIALS

■ 2 3½oz/100g hanks (each approx 120yd/110m) of Trendsetter Yarns *Segue* (nylon) in #602 country meadow (A)
■ 5 1¾oz/50g balls (each approx 80yd/73m) of Trendsetter Yarns *Dune* (mohair/acrylic/nylon) in #100 centurion (B)
■ One pair size 11 (8mm) needles *or size to obtain gauge*

GAUGE

9¾ sts and 12 rows to 4"/10cm over pat st using size 11 (8mm) needles.
Take time to check gauge.

WRAP

With A, cast on 56 sts. Change to B. Cont in pat st as foll:

Rows 1–10 Knit. Change to A.

Rows 11 and 12 Knit.

Row 13 (RS) K6, *yo twice, k1, yo 3 times, k1, yo 4 times, k1, yo 3 times, k1, yo twice, k6; rep from * to end.

Row 14 Knit across, dropping extra wraps.

Rows 15 and 16 Knit. Change to B.

Rows 17–24 Knit. Change to A.

Rows 25 and 26 Knit.

Row 27 K1, *yo twice, k1, yo 3 times, k1, yo 4 times, k1, yo 3 times, k1, yo twice, k6; rep from *, end last rep k1 instead of k6.

Row 28 Knit across, dropping extra wraps.

Rows 29 and 30 Knit. Change to B. Rep rows 1–30 5 times more, then rows 1–10 once. Bind off all sts knitwise using A.

MULTI-YARN WRAP
Special blend

■■□▷

Barry Klein combined nine beautiful yarns using a clever striping technique to produce bold gradations of colors and textures.

SIZES

Instructions are written for one size.

KNITTED MEASUREMENTS

■ Approx 22"/56cm wide x 66"/167.5cm long

MATERIALS

■ 1 .88oz/25g ball (approx 62yd/57m) of Trendsetter Yarns *Joy* (polyamide/polyester) in #1830 pink zebra (A) ⬛

■ 1 1¾oz/50g ball (approx 80yd/73m) of Trendsetter Yarns *Pandora Shadow* (polyamide) in #1775 rose blossoms (B) ⬛

■ 1 1¾oz/50g ball (approx 100yd/91m) of Trendsetter Yarns *Magique* (polyamide/cotton/acrylic/polyester) in #6070 purple, plums & plumaria (C) ⬛

■ 1 1¾oz/50g ball (approx 72yd/66m) of Trendsetter Yarns *Zucca* (nylon/polyamide) in #5034 plum (D) ⬛

■ 1 1¾oz/50g ball (approx 65yd/59m) of Trendsetter Yarns *Madison* (acrylic/wool) in #14 wine tweed (E) ⬛

■ 1 1¾oz/50g hank (approx 80yd/73m) of Trendsetter Yarns *Cristal* (polyamide) in #410 wine barrel (F) ⬛

■ 1 1¾oz/50g ball (approx 145yd/133m) of Trendsetter Yarns *Aura* (nylon) in #9322 rust (G) ⬛

■ 1 1¾oz/50g skein (approx 80yd/73m) of Trendsetter Yarns *Bazaar* (viscose/linen/polyester) in #77 sun burst (H) ⬛

■ 1 1¾oz/50g ball (approx 80yd/73m) of Trendsetter Yarns *Dune* (mohair/acrylic/nylon) in #97 rusty rasta (I) ⬛

■ One pair size 10 (6mm) needles *or size to obtain gauge*

GAUGE

11 sts to 4"/10cm over corrugated rib using size 10 (6mm) needles.
Take time to check gauge.

CORRUGATED RIB PATTERN

Row 1 (RS) Knit.
Rows 2 and 3 Purl.
Row 4 Knit.
Rep rows 1–4 for corrugated rib.

COLOR SEQUENCE

The wrap is made using 3 yarns at a time; beg with A, B and C. Using a single strand of each yarn throughout, work in corrugated rib, alternating the 3 colors every row. Carry colors not in use along side edge of work, taking care that edge lies flat. When color A runs out, join color D and cont to alternate colors in order as established. When color B runs out, join color E, and when color C runs out, join color F. Cont to join yarns as needed foll the color order to the end.

With A, loosely cast on 60 sts. Beg with B, cont in corrugated rib and color sequence, until piece measures 66"/167.5cm from beg, end with a WS row. Bind off all sts loosely knitwise.

■■■◻

Every summer wardrobe needs something smart for covering up when nights get breezy. The perfect choice is Kathy Zimmerman's pretty peek-a-boo pattern shawl.

SIZES

Instructions are written for one size.

KNITTED MEASUREMENTS

■ Approx 18"/45.5cm wide x 68"/172.5cm long

MATERIALS

■ 10 1¾oz/50g balls (each approx 110yd/100m) of Nashua Handknits/Westminster Fibers, Inc., *Natural Focus Ecologie* (naturally dyed pima cotton) in #80 chestnut (4)

■ Two size 5 (3.75mm) circular needles, 24"/60cm long *or size to obtain gauge*

■ One size 5 (3.75cm) needle (for three-needle bind-off)

■ Stitch markers

GAUGE

21 sts and 32 rows to 4"/10cm over wave and leaf pat st using size 5 (3.75mm) circular needle.
Take time to check gauge.

Note

Shawl is made in 2 halves, then joined tog using three-needle bind-off.

WAVE AND LEAF PATTERN STITCH

(multiple of 10 sts plus 5)

Row 1 (RS) K2, *yo, ssk, k8; rep from * to last 3 sts, end yo, ssk, k1.

Row 2 P3, *yo, p2tog, p5, p2tog tbl, yo, p1; rep from * to last 2 sts, end p2.

Row 3 K2, *k2, yo, ssk, k3, k2tog, yo, k1; rep from * to last 3 sts, end k3.

Row 4 P3, *p2, yo, p2tog, p1, p2tog tbl, yo, p3; rep from * to last 2 sts, end p2.

Row 5 K2, *k4, yo, SK2P, yo, k3; rep from * to last 3 sts, end k3.

Row 6 Purl.

Row 7 K2, k2tog, *yo twice, ssk, k3, k2tog, yo twice, SK2P; rep from * to last 4 sts, end yo twice, ssk, k2.

Row 8 P3, *work (p1, k1) in the 2 yo's, p5, work (k1, p1) in the 2 yo's, p1; rep from * to last 2 sts, end p2.

Row 9 K2, *k2, yo twice, SK2P, k1, k3tog, yo twice, k1; rep from * to last 3 sts, end k3.

Row 10 P3, *p1, work (p1, k1) in the 2 yo's, p3, work (k1, p1) in the 2 yo's, p2; rep from * to last 2 sts, end p2.

Row 11 K2, *k3, yo twice, (sl 2, k3tog, p2sso)—*S2K3P2 made*, yo twice, k2; rep from * to last 3 sts, end k3.

Row 12 P3, *p2, work (k1, p1) in the 2 yo's, p1, work (p1, k1) in the 2 yo's, p3; rep from * to last 2 sts, end p2.

Row 13 K2, *k1, k3tog, yo twice, k3, yo twice, SK2P; rep from * to last 3 sts, end k3.

Row 14 P3, *p1, work (k1, p1) in the 2 yo's, p3, work (p1, k1) in the 2 yo's, p2; rep from * to last 2 sts, end p2.

Row 15 K2, k3tog, *yo twice, K5, yo twice, S2K3P2; rep from * to last 5 sts, end yo twice, SK2P, k2.

Row 16 P3, *work (k1, p1) in the 2 yo's, p5, work (p1, k1) in the 2 yo's, p1; rep from * to last 2 sts, end p2.

Row 17 K2, *k5, yo, ssk, k3; rep from * to last 3 sts, end k3.

Row 18 P3, *p2, p2tog tbl, yo, p1, yo, p2tog, p3; rep from * to last 2 sts, end p2.

Row 19 K2, *k2, k2tog, yo, k3, yo, ssk, k1; rep from * to last 3 sts, end k3.

Row 20 P3, *p2tog tbl, yo, p5, yo, p2tog, p1; rep from * to last 2 sts, end p2.

Row 21 K2, k2tog, *yo, k7, yo, SK2P; rep from * to last 4 sts, end ssk, k2.

Row 22 Purl.

Row 23 K2, *k2, k2tog, yo twice, SK2P, yo twice, ssk, k1; rep from * to last 3 sts, end k3.

Row 24 Rep row 12.

Row 25 K2, *k1, k3tog, yo twice, k3, yo twice, SK2P; rep from * to last 3 sts, end k3.

Row 26 Rep row 14.

Row 27 K2, k3tog, *yo twice, k5, yo twice, S2K3P2, p2sso; rep from * to last 5 sts, end yo twice, SK2P, k2.

Row 28 Rep row 8.

Row 29 K2, *k2, yo twice, SK2P, k1, k3tog, yo twice, k1; rep from * to last 3 sts, end k3.

Row 30 Rep row 10.

Row 31 K2, *k3, yo twice, S2K3P2, yo twice, k2; rep from * to last 3 sts, end k3.

Row 32 P3, *p2, work (p1, k1) in the 2

yo's, p1, work (k1, p1) in the 2 yo's, p3; rep from * to last 2 sts, end p2.

Rep rows 1–32 for wave and leaf pat st.

SHAWL

First half

With circular needle. cast on 95 sts. Do not join. Working back and forth, knit 3 rows.

Next row (RS) K5, pm, work row 1 of wave and leaf pat st over center 85 sts, pm, k5.

Next row K5, sl marker, work row 2 of wave and leaf pat st over center 85 sts, sl marker, k5. Keeping 5 sts each side in garter st, cont to work as foll: work rows 3-6 once, rows 1–6 once, rows 1–32 seven times, then rows 1–27 once, end WS.

Piece measures approx 33"/84cm from beg.

Leave sts on needle.

Second half

Work as for first half.

FINISHING

Block pieces lightly to measurements.

JOINING

With RS tog, hold shawl halves on two parallel circular needles. Insert straight needle knitwise into first st of each needle and wrap yarn around each needle as if to knit. Knit these 2 sts tog and sl them off the needles. *K the next 2 sts tog in the same manner. Sl first st on straight needle over the 2nd st and off the needle. Rep from * across row until all sts are bound off.

Wave and Leaf Pattern Chart

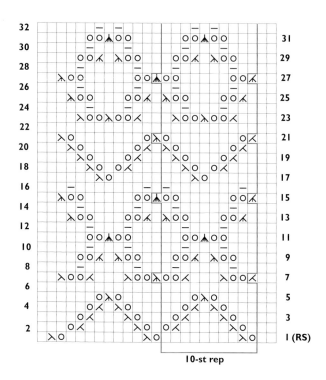

10-st rep

Stitch Key

K on RS, P on WS

P on RS, K on WS

Yo

SSK on RS, p2tog-tbl on WS

K2tog on RS, p2tog on WS

SK2P - Sl1, k2tog, psso

K3tog on RS, p3tog on WS

S2K3P2 - Sl2tog knitwise, k3tog, p2sso

FLOWERS AND
SNOWFLAKES SHAWL
Blue Danube

Debbie O'Neill has paired two winter-themed lace patterns—frost flowers and snowflakes—to create an elegant shawl that's perfect any time of the year.

SIZES
Instructions are written for one size.

KNITTED MEASUREMENTS
■ Approx 19"/48cm wide x 76"/193cm long

MATERIALS
■ 1 4oz/113g hank (each approx 1250yd/1143m) of Lorna's Laces *Helen's Lace* (silk/wool) in #37ns violet ⬛
■ Two pairs size 4 (3.5mm) needles *or size to obtain gauge*

GAUGE
23 sts and 27 rows to 4"/10cm over chart pats using size 4 (3.5mm) needles (after blocking).
Take time to check gauge.

Note
Shawl is made in 2 panels, then grafted tog.

PANEL 1
Cast on 110 sts loosely.

Beg chart 1
Row 1 (RS) Beg with st 1 and work to st 38, rep sts 5–38 twice, then work sts 39 to 42—110 sts. Cont to foll chart in this manner to row 24, then rep rows 1–24 3 times more, then rows 1–12 once. Cont as foll:
Row 1 (RS) Knit.
Row 2 K4, p to last 4 sts, end k4.
Row 3 K4, *yo, k2tog; rep from * to last 4 sts, end k4.
Row 4 K4, p to last 4 sts, end k4.
Row 5 K4, *k2tog, yo; rep from * to last 6 sts, end k2tog, k4—109 sts.
Row 6 K4, p to last 4 sts, end k4. Piece should measure approx 17"/43cm from beg. Leave sts on needle. Cut yarn, leaving a 2yd/2m tail for grafting.

PANEL 2
Work chart 1 as for panel 1, then row rows 1–6.
Row 7 Knit.
Beg chart 2
Row 1 (WS) Beg with st 1 and work to st 16, rep sts 9–16 11 times, then work sts 17 to 21—109 sts. Cont to foll chart in this manner to row 12, then rep rows 1–12 until piece measures 59"/150cm from beg, end with a WS row. Knit next row. Leave sts on needle.

JOINING PANELS
Graft the 2 panels tog using Kitchener stitch. Place panel 1 in front of panel 2, WS facing and needle tips pointing to the right. Thread tail in tapestry needle. Insert tapestry needle into first st on front needle as if to purl, then pull yarn through, leaving st on needle. Insert the needle into the first stitch on the back needle as if to knit, then pull

yarn through, leaving st on needle. Cont as foll:

Step 1 Insert needle into first st on front needle as if to knit and slip it off needle.

Step 2 Insert needle into next st on front needle as if to purl, then pull yarn through leaving st on needle.

Step 3 Insert needle into first st on back needle as if to purl and slip it off needle.

Step 4 Insert needle into next st on back needle as if to knit, then pull yarn through leaving st on needle. Taking care to maintain gauge, rep steps 1–4 until you have grafted all sts, rep steps 1 and 2 for the garter st borders.

FINISHING

Block piece to measurements.

Chart 1—Frost Flowers Pattern

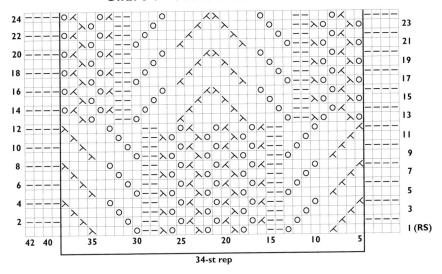

34-st rep

Chart 2—Snowflakes Pattern

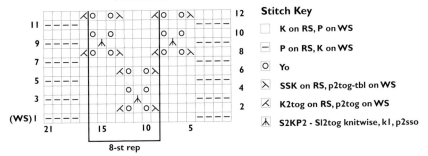

8-st rep

Stitch Key

☐	K on RS, P on WS
—	P on RS, K on WS
O	Yo
⅄	SSK on RS, p2tog-tbl on WS
⋌	K2tog on RS, p2tog on WS
人	S2KP2 - Sl2tog knitwise, k1, p2sso

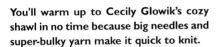

You'll warm up to Cecily Glowik's cozy shawl in no time because big needles and super-bulky yarn make it quick to knit.

Instructions are written for one size.

KNITTED MEASUREMENTS
■ Approx 14"/35.5cm wide x 65"/165cm long *(excluding fringe)*

MATERIALS
■ 8 3½oz/100g hanks (each approx 45yd/41m) of Blue Sky Alpacas *Bulky Hand Dyes* (alpaca/wool) in #1011 teal ⑥
■ One pair size 15 (10mm) needles *or size to obtain gauge*

GAUGE
9 sts and 6 rows to 4"/10cm over drop st pat using size 15 (10mm) needles.
Take time to check gauge.

DROP-STITCH PATTERN
(multiple of 4 sts)
Row 1 (WS) Purl across wrapping yarn twice around needle for each st.
Row 2 *Sl next 4 sts to RH needle dropping extra wraps and forming 4 elongated sts, sl these 4 sts back to LH needle, working through all 4 sts at once, work [k4tog, p4tog] twice; rep from * to end.
Row 3 P2, purl across wrapping yarn twice around needle for each st, to the last 2 sts, end p2.
Row 4 K2, *sl next 4 sts to RH needle dropping extra wraps and forming 4 elongated sts, sl these 4 sts back to LH needle, working through all 4 sts at once, work [k4tog, p4tog] twice; rep from *, end k2.
Rep rows 1–4 for drop st pat.

SHAWL
Cast on 32 sts. Work in drop st pat until piece measures 65"/165cm from beg, end with a RS row. Bind off all sts purlwise.

FINISHING
Block piece to measurements.

FRINGE
Cut 42 stands 16"/40.5cm long. Using 3 strands for each fringe, attach 7 fringes evenly spaced across each end of shawl. Trim ends evenly.

RESOURCES

U.S. RESOURCES

Write to the yarn companies listed below for purchasing and mail-order information.

Alchemy Yarns of Transformation
P.O. Box 1080
Sebastopol, CA 95473
www.alchemyyarns.com

Artyarns
39 Westmoreland Avenue
White Plains, NY 10606
www.artyarns.com

Berroco, Inc.
P.O. Box 367
14 Elmdale Road
Uxbridge, MA 01569
www.berroco.com

Blue Sky Alpacas
P.O. Box 88
Cedar, MN 55011
www.blueskyalpacas.com

Classic Elite Yarns
122 Western Avenue
Lowell, MA 01851
www.classiceliteyarns.com

Coats & Clark
P.O. Box 12229
Greenville, SC 29612
www.coatsandclark.com

Dale of Norway
4750 Shelburne Road
Shelburne, VT 05482
www.dale.no

Fiber Trends
P.O. Box 7266
East Wenatchee, WA 98802
www.fibertrends.com

Ironstone Yarns
5401 San Diego Rd. NE
Albuquerque, NM 87113
www.ironstoneonline.com

Jade Sapphire Exotic Fibres
866-857-3897
www.jadesapphire.com

Knit One, Crochet Too, Inc.
91 Tandberg Trail, Unit 6
Windham, ME 04062
www.knitonecrochettoo.com

Kolláge Yarns
3304 Blue Bell Lane
Birmingham, AL 35242
www.kollageyarns.com

Lorna's Laces
4229 North Honore Street
Chicago, IL 60613
www.lornaslaces.net

Malabrigo Yarn
786-866-6187
www.malabrigoyarn.com

Moda Dea
distributed by
Coats & Clark
www.modadea.com

Nashua Handknits
distributed by
Westminster Fibers, Inc.

Naturally NZ
distributed by
Fiber Trends

Prism Yarns
3140 39th Ave. North
St. Petersburg FL 33714
www.prismyarn.com

The Schaefer Yarn Company
3514 Kelly's Corners Rd.
Interlaken, NY 14847
www.schaeferyarn.com

Tilli Tomas
72 Woodland Road
Boston MA 02130
www.tillitomas.com

Trendsetter Yarns
16745 Saticoy Street,
Suite #101
Van Nuys, CA 91406
www.trendsetteryarns.com

Westminster Fibers, Inc.
4 Townsend Avenue, Unit 8
Nashua, NH 03063
www.westminsterfibers.com